HALLOWEEN

ACTIVITY BOOK

FOR KIDS

HALLOWEEN
Word Search

Disclaimer

The puzzles, games and activities in this book are for entertainment purposes only. although the author and publisher have worked very hard to ensure that the information in this book is accurate, the rader should be aware that errors and or omissions may occur. the author and publisher disclaime any lability to any person or party for any loss resulting from reliance on any information in this book.

This Book Belongs To

CALoRING

ABC PATH

ABC Path consists of a 5x5 grid. Around the edges of the grid are the letters B to Y. The letter A has been placed.

- The goal is to fill in all the cells so that all letters A to Y appear exactly once.

- Each letter must appear in the row, column, or diagonal corresponding to its clue.

- Each letter must be a neighbor to the letter that comes before and after it.

ABC PATH - 1

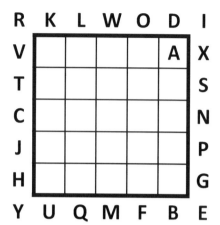

ABC PATH - 2

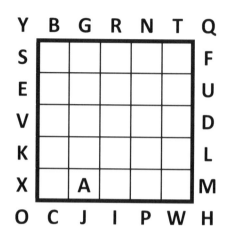

ABC PATH - 3

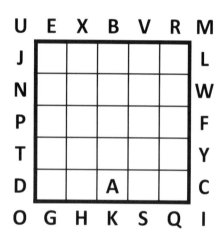

ABC PATH - 4

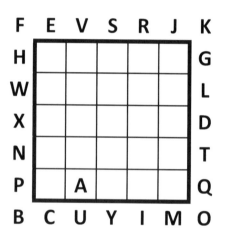

ABC PATH - 5

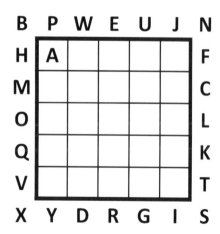

ABC PATH - 6

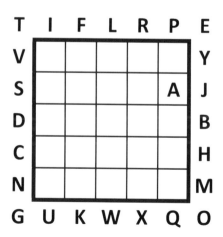

ABC PATH - 7

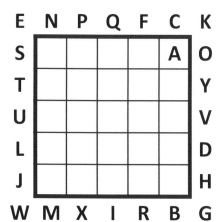

ABC PATH - 8

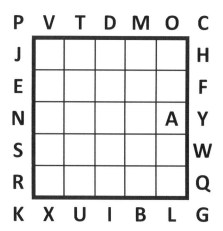

ABC PATH - 9

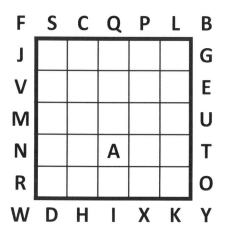

ABC PATH - 10

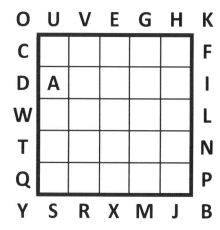

ABC PATH - 11

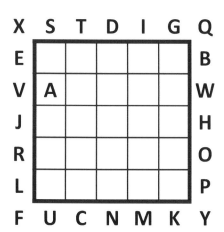

ABC PATH - 12

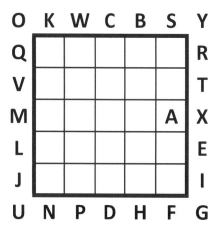

ABC PATH - 13

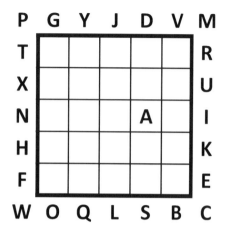

ABC PATH - 14

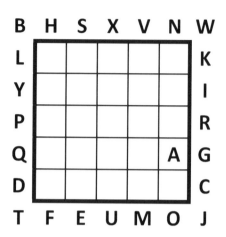

ABC PATH - 15

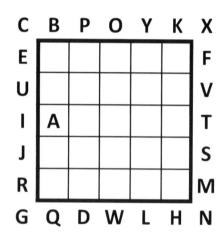

ABC PATH - 16

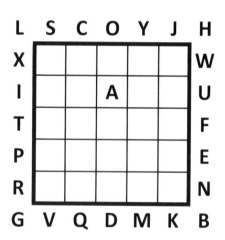

ABC PATH - 17

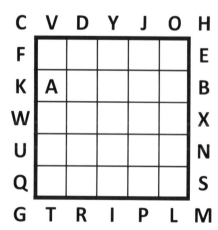

ABC PATH - 18

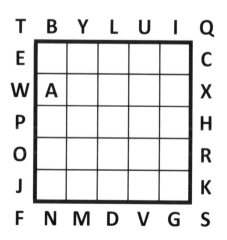

ABC PATH - 1 (Solution)

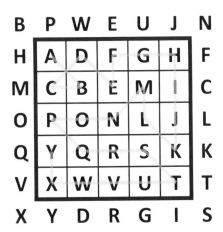

```
  R  K  L  W  O  D  I
V | U  V  W  X  A | X
T | T  S  M  Y  B | S
C | K  L  R  N  C | N
J | J  Q  P  O  D | P
H | I  H  G  F  E | G
  Y  U  Q  M  F  B  E
```

ABC PATH - 2 (Solution)

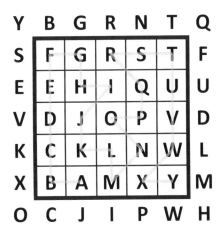

```
  Y  B  G  R  N  T  Q
S | F  G  R  S  T | F
E | E  H  I  Q  U | U
V | D  J  O  P  V | D
K | C  K  L  N  W | L
X | B  A  M  X  Y | M
  O  C  J  I  P  W  H
```

ABC PATH - 3 (Solution)

```
  U  E  X  B  V  R  M
J | I  J  K  L  M | L
N | G  H  W  O  N | W
P | F  X  U  V  P | F
T | E  Y  B  T  Q | Y
D | D  C  A  S  R | C
  O  G  H  K  S  Q  I
```

ABC PATH - 4 (Solution)

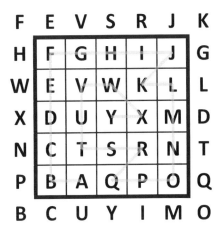

```
  F  E  V  S  R  J  K
H | F  G  H  I  J | G
W | E  V  W  K  L | L
X | D  U  Y  X  M | D
N | C  T  S  R  N | T
P | B  A  Q  P  O | Q
  B  C  U  Y  I  M  O
```

ABC PATH - 5 (Solution)

```
  B  P  W  E  U  J  N
H | A  D  F  G  H | F
M | C  B  E  M  I | C
O | P  O  N  L  J | L
Q | Y  Q  R  S  K | K
V | X  W  V  U  T | T
  X  Y  D  R  G  I  S
```

ABC PATH - 6 (Solution)

```
  T  I  F  L  R  P  E
V | U  V  W  X  Y | Y
S | J  T  S  R  A | J
D | I  K  D  B  Q | B
C | H  E  L  C  P | H
N | G  F  M  N  O | M
  G  U  K  W  X  Q  O
```

ABC PATH - 7 (Solution)

```
    E  N  P  Q  F  C  K
 S | O  P  Q  S  A | O
 T | N  Y  T  R  B | Y
 U | M  X  V  U  C | V
 L | L  W  I  G  D | D
 J | K  J  H  F  E | H
    W  M  X  I  R  B  G
```

ABC PATH - 8 (Solution)

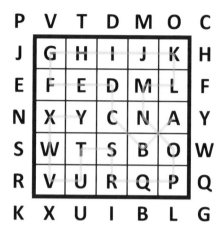

```
    P  V  T  D  M  O  C
 J | G  H  I  J  K | H
 E | F  E  D  M  L | F
 N | X  Y  C  N  A | Y
 S | W  T  S  B  O | W
 R | V  U  R  Q  P | Q
    K  X  U  I  B  L  G
```

ABC PATH - 9 (Solution)

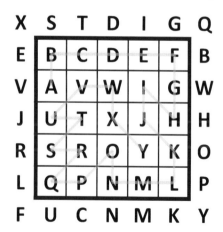

```
    F  S  C  Q  P  L  B
 J | F  G  I  J  K | G
 V | E  H  V  W  L | E
 M | D  U  B  X  M | U
 N | T  C  A  Y  N | T
 R | S  R  Q  P  O | O
    W  D  H  I  X  K  Y
```

ABC PATH - 10 (Solution)

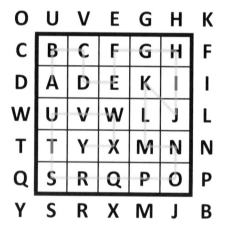

```
    O  U  V  E  G  H  K
 C | B  C  F  G  H | F
 D | A  D  E  K  I | I
 W | U  V  W  L  J | L
 T | T  Y  X  M  N | N
 Q | S  R  Q  P  O | P
    Y  S  R  X  M  J  B
```

ABC PATH - 11 (Solution)

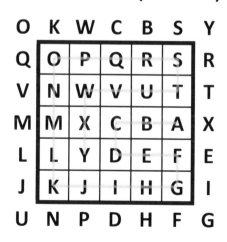

```
    X  S  T  D  I  G  Q
 E | B  C  D  E  F | B
 V | A  V  W  I  G | W
 J | U  T  X  J  H | H
 R | S  R  O  Y  K | O
 L | Q  P  N  M  L | P
    F  U  C  N  M  K  Y
```

ABC PATH - 12 (Solution)

```
    O  K  W  C  B  S  Y
 Q | O  P  Q  R  S | R
 V | N  W  V  U  T | T
 M | M  X  C  B  A | X
 L | L  Y  D  E  F | E
 J | K  J  I  H  G | I
    U  N  P  D  H  F  G
```

ABC PATH - 13 (Solution)

```
    P  G  Y  J  D  V  M
T |  P  Q  R  S  T | R
X |  O  Y  X  W  U | U
N |  N  I  J  A  V | I
H |  H  M  L  K  B | K
F |  G  F  E  D  C | E
    W  O  Q  L  S  B  C
```

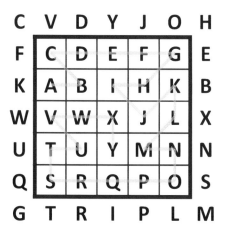

ABC PATH - 14 (Solution)

```
    B  H  S  X  V  N  W
L |  J  K  L  M  N | K
Y |  I  Y  X  W  O | I
P |  H  S  R  V  P | R
Q |  G  T  U  Q  A | G
D |  F  E  D  C  B | C
    T  F  E  U  M  O  J
```

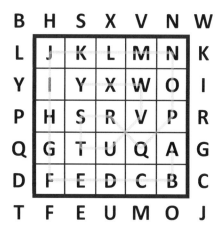

ABC PATH - 15 (Solution)

```
    C  B  P  O  Y  K  X
E |  C  D  E  F  G | F
U |  B  U  V  X  H | V
I |  A  T  W  Y  I | T
J |  Q  S  O  N  J | S
R |  R  P  M  L  K | M
    G  Q  D  W  L  H  N
```

ABC PATH - 16 (Solution)

```
    L  S  C  O  Y  J  H
X |  V  W  X  Y  H | W
I |  U  B  A  G  I | U
T |  T  C  D  F  J | F
P |  S  P  O  E  K | E
R |  R  Q  N  M  L | N
    G  V  Q  D  M  K  B
```

ABC PATH - 17 (Solution)

```
    C  V  D  Y  J  O  H
F |  C  D  E  F  G | E
K |  A  B  I  H  K | B
W |  V  W  X  J  L | X
U |  T  U  Y  M  N | N
Q |  S  R  Q  P  O | S
    G  T  R  I  P  L  M
```

ABC PATH - 18 (Solution)

```
    T  B  Y  L  U  I  Q
E |  B  C  D  E  F | C
W |  A  X  W  V  G | X
P |  P  Y  S  U  H | H
O |  O  Q  R  T  I | R
J |  N  M  L  K  J | K
    F  N  M  D  V  G  S
```

WORD SEARCH

A word search puzzle is a word game that consists of the letters of words placed in a grid, which usually has a rectangular or square shape.

The objective of this puzzle is to find and mark all the words hidden inside the box.

The words may be placed horizontally, vertically, or diagonally.

Often a list of the hidden words is provided, but more challenging puzzles may not provide a list.

Many word search puzzles have a theme to which all the hidden words are related such as food, animals, or colors.

Halloween Word Search for Kids 49

```
T  A  R  S  H  U  B  P  I  Z  V  X  Y  V  O  G  X  E
P  W  T  E  D  L  L  G  F  B  L  S  X  A  Z  R  U  R
X  D  O  I  O  R  E  E  J  K  F  R  B  H  P  A  A  X
Y  O  G  M  L  T  K  T  R  I  L  N  M  H  H  V  L  Z
X  N  O  O  G  O  B  D  J  G  X  G  X  L  Y  E  F  M
W  R  T  G  I  U  L  G  C  O  N  Y  Q  Y  M  Y  M  P
J  G  H  G  S  L  Y  C  R  T  H  X  I  U  A  A  Y  A
C  C  I  J  R  H  U  I  I  E  D  T  T  G  G  R  K  K
D  U  C  W  I  A  X  I  L  H  E  V  D  V  H  D  M  F
K  T  N  H  E  V  V  P  E  G  T  N  I  Y  B  D  H  C
F  U  O  Y  P  Q  Y  E  D  T  K  O  Q  G  L  I  L  R
Q  O  V  N  W  Z  Q  V  D  N  S  N  G  X  A  R  L  C
S  C  E  U  E  K  K  B  T  I  P  N  I  A  V  T  W  G
P  B  L  N  W  J  W  A  G  N  G  F  Y  M  N  C  H  K
G  R  A  V  E  M  A  R  K  E  R  G  U  L  H  U  F  K
D  M  R  E  Q  V  A  G  R  E  M  L  I  N  S  P  L  X
Z  A  J  G  H  S  R  G  S  Y  L  Z  E  N  Z  S  B  T
G  R  A  V  E  Y  A  R  D  S  H  I  F  T  G  C  P  S
```

Halloween Word List

Gothic Lolita
Gothic novel
Grave digging
Grave marker

Graveyard Dirt Cups
Graveyard shift
Green
Gremlins

Halloween Word Search for Kids 50

```
H  J  L  A  A  B  I  D  R  B  T  L  D  Q  J  L  O  Q
H  G  N  X  X  W  T  X  M  P  J  J  X  N  M  X  S  Z
T  A  R  G  R  I  M  A  C  E  A  U  B  G  L  A  J  A
O  A  B  I  B  Y  E  U  K  H  B  L  R  O  P  I  J  V
I  L  E  U  M  Y  L  M  I  R  G  I  S  R  A  S  W  S
E  M  F  I  R  A  M  D  A  P  F  M  E  E  S  W  X  I
G  M  Y  N  J  R  C  J  P  F  K  U  T  L  L  W  A  J
R  W  V  L  F  H  M  I  I  Y  Q  N  A  H  T  Y  E  D
I  H  L  U  Y  Z  D  N  N  S  C  L  Q  S  G  I  V  W
M  V  C  Z  C  K  R  Q  E  G  H  O  D  E  B  K  G  C
O  N  K  A  I  F  D  T  G  J  P  E  D  J  Y  R  M  Q
I  H  K  I  P  K  O  S  W  T  L  U  Z  Z  B  O  V  S
R  U  M  B  Q  R  U  E  V  X  A  O  M  O  X  Y  O  T
E  U  N  J  G  L  J  W  F  J  V  H  Q  P  Y  E  J  U
C  J  Z  C  I  G  T  R  X  F  F  D  K  D  K  G  Z  K
G  R  I  M  R  E  A  P  E  R  A  D  G  I  T  I  F  H
O  O  W  G  H  P  I  S  U  U  A  M  P  X  J  D  N  N
G  X  C  W  O  C  V  V  S  B  C  P  N  Y  D  F  O  D
```

Halloween Word List

Griffin

Grim Reaper

Grimace

Grimacing Pumpkin

Grimly

Grimoire

Grotesque

Halloween Word Search for Kids 51

```
B H F A B L Z H A N G I N G B A T S
V G R O T E S Q U E R I E F S A X H
Z B L B B V B L P X D N L H E S K A
G K A E R V A Q M H J D S S I L X N
C H K A Q C E P A F P C K S T L T G
K R A K I L C S R P I I V P R A O I
V X F R E G K G X U F X B F A B I N
H I Q W C F M R H U D F A G P E X G
B A J P Z B Y U D F Q U G S N Y V S
A P I U K D S E M J U G Z M E E R K
K U H R E V S L G T I Z R E Y T E
F F U F R K W O O B F G O O W M G L
B S Z S J A S M K A Q Q D W O M N E
B Z Q Q Z L I E D E D H O Y L U B T
X D V E I T O S N V K A X M L G W O
I L R O C I X M I S N P S M A S C N
Z R H D C P E C H N Q T Q U H J A S
D F E Y T O X A B N G W E G Q B Y F
```

Halloween Word List

Grotesquerie
Gruesome
Gummy Eyeballs
Gummy Worms

Hair-Raising
Halloween Parties
Hanging Bats
Hanging Skeletons

Halloween Word Search for Kids 52

```
S  W  W  U  Z  W  X  I  Y  S  P  L  U  C  J  O  L  X
L  F  F  O  H  A  R  A  S  S  M  E  N  T  O  O  T  A
A  C  I  N  F  D  M  I  G  D  M  X  H  J  G  M  T  Q
V  J  W  E  C  A  F  O  E  R  H  V  F  I  L  N  M  C
I  H  Z  Y  K  A  D  F  W  I  O  U  F  V  N  F  C  D
T  R  A  F  S  P  R  K  T  U  C  K  K  O  P  V  G  T
S  I  S  P  H  Z  N  V  W  U  J  F  W  M  E  Z  K  J
E  J  V  G  P  C  A  D  L  H  A  R  B  I  N  G  E  R
F  H  G  Y  W  Y  Y  J  P  N  S  X  Z  S  D  Y  A  R
T  A  I  S  U  W  H  V  B  P  L  C  J  T  D  H  D  D
S  T  S  V  M  U  A  A  S  V  U  Y  A  A  D  Q  M  M
E  E  S  M  B  K  S  T  U  V  I  M  Z  G  T  B  O  U
V  F  A  L  W  L  C  H  N  G  Y  L  Z  N  P  G  K
R  U  R  H  D  V  U  A  A  O  T  T  T  C  U  E  J  X
A  L  A  I  T  O  W  G  R  I  C  I  N  G  A  C  J  T
H  Y  H  F  X  D  P  A  P  F  W  G  N  K  H  H  W  I
V  I  F  Y  F  W  V  Q  Y  I  W  G  M  G  F  W  S  P
S  R  U  J  D  C  M  E  D  Z  V  J  A  R  M  Q  L  P
```

Halloween Word List

Happy Haunting
Harass
Harassment
Harbinger

Harpy
Harvest Festivals
Hateful
Haunt

Halloween Word Search for Kids 49

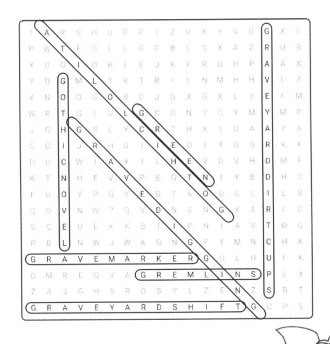

Halloween Word Search for Kids 50

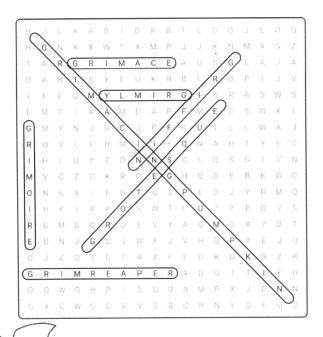

Halloween Word Search for Kids 51

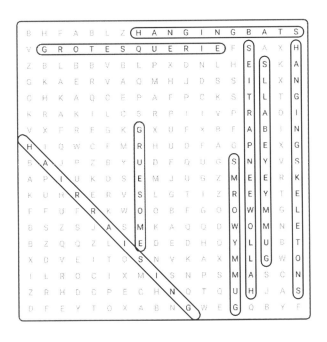

Halloween Word Search for Kids 52

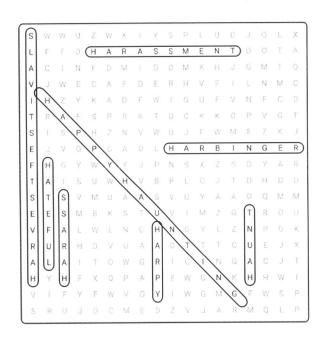

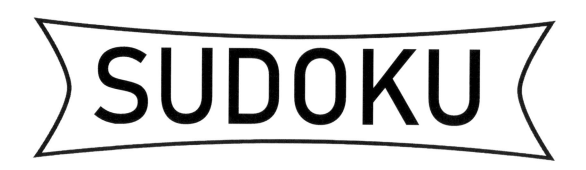

SUDOKU

Sudoku is 9x9 (classic, adult version), or 4x4 and 6x6 (kids versions) grid puzzle game.

In the adult version, the objective is to fill the 9×9 grid with digits so that each column, each row, and each of the nine 3×3 subgrids that compose the grid (also called "boxes", "blocks", or "regions") contain all of the digits from 1 to 9.

You are provided a partially completed puzzle to complete, with a single solution.

In the adult version, 4 difficulty levels can be found, Easy, Intermediate, Hard and Insane.

SUDOKU - 1

Kids (6 x 6)

1			2		3
	4	3	6		
4	3	1		6	
6				1	4
	1		4	2	5
5		4	1		

SUDOKU - 2

Kids (6 x 6)

	2		4		5
		5		6	3
5	3	4			
6	1			3	4
4	6		3	5	
2		3	6		

SUDOKU - 3

Kids (6 x 6)

	4		5		2
	1	2	4	3	
2			6		1
	6	4		2	
4			2	6	
6	2	3			4

SUDOKU - 4

Kids (6 x 6)

3		4		2	
6	5	2	1		
	3		2	5	1
		5	6		4
	6	3	4		
2				6	5

SUDOKU - 5

Kids (6 x 6)

		3	4	6	5
4	5			3	
		4	6		1
	6			5	4
6		5	2		
3	2	1		4	

SUDOKU - 6

Kids (6 x 6)

	4			1	2
	5		4	3	
	6	5		2	3
2		3	6		
5	3		2		1
6		1		5	

SUDOKU - 7

Kids (6 x 6)

		4	5	6	
5	6				4
			4	5	1
4		1			6
1	3	6	2		
2	4			1	3

SUDOKU - 8

Kids (6 x 6)

	3	5			2
	4	6		5	1
4	5			6	
	6		5	1	4
5		4	1		
6			4	2	

SUDOKU - 9

Kids (6 x 6)

2			5	6	
	1			4	3
3	2			1	5
		5	4		2
	3	2	1		
6	5	1		2	

SUDOKU - 10

Kids (6 x 6)

1		3		6	
	6		3	1	
2	5				3
3			6	2	5
4		5	2		6
	3	2			1

SUDOKU - 11

Kids (6 x 6)

5	2		6		3
6			2	4	5
3		6	1		
	1	2			6
		3		6	2
	6		4	3	

SUDOKU - 12

Kids (6 x 6)

	3			2	6
6	5		4		
		6	1		3
4	1			6	
3		1		5	2
2	6	5	3		

SUDOKU - 1 (Solution)
Kids (6 x 6)

1	6	5	2	4	3
2	4	3	6	5	1
4	3	1	5	6	2
6	5	2	3	1	4
3	1	6	4	2	5
5	2	4	1	3	6

SUDOKU - 2 (Solution)
Kids (6 x 6)

3	2	6	4	1	5
1	4	5	2	6	3
5	3	4	1	2	6
6	1	2	5	3	4
4	6	1	3	5	2
2	5	3	6	4	1

SUDOKU - 3 (Solution)
Kids (6 x 6)

3	4	6	5	1	2
5	1	2	4	3	6
2	3	5	6	4	1
1	6	4	3	2	5
4	5	1	2	6	3
6	2	3	1	5	4

SUDOKU - 4 (Solution)
Kids (6 x 6)

3	1	4	5	2	6
6	5	2	1	4	3
4	3	6	2	5	1
1	2	5	6	3	4
5	6	3	4	1	2
2	4	1	3	6	5

SUDOKU - 5 (Solution)

Kids (6 x 6)

2	1	3	4	6	5
4	5	6	1	3	2
5	3	4	6	2	1
1	6	2	3	5	4
6	4	5	2	1	3
3	2	1	5	4	6

SUDOKU - 6 (Solution)

Kids (6 x 6)

3	4	6	5	1	2
1	5	2	4	3	6
4	6	5	1	2	3
2	1	3	6	4	5
5	3	4	2	6	1
6	2	1	3	5	4

SUDOKU - 7 (Solution)

Kids (6 x 6)

3	1	4	5	6	2
5	6	2	1	3	4
6	2	3	4	5	1
4	5	1	3	2	6
1	3	6	2	4	5
2	4	5	6	1	3

SUDOKU - 8 (Solution)

Kids (6 x 6)

1	3	5	6	4	2
2	4	6	3	5	1
4	5	1	2	6	3
3	6	2	5	1	4
5	2	4	1	3	6
6	1	3	4	2	5

SUDOKU - 9 (Solution)

Kids (6 x 6)

2	4	3	5	6	1
5	1	6	2	4	3
3	2	4	6	1	5
1	6	5	4	3	2
4	3	2	1	5	6
6	5	1	3	2	4

SUDOKU - 10 (Solution)

Kids (6 x 6)

1	2	3	5	6	4
5	6	4	3	1	2
2	5	6	1	4	3
3	4	1	6	2	5
4	1	5	2	3	6
6	3	2	4	5	1

SUDOKU - 11 (Solution)

Kids (6 x 6)

5	2	4	6	1	3
6	3	1	2	4	5
3	5	6	1	2	4
4	1	2	3	5	6
1	4	3	5	6	2
2	6	5	4	3	1

SUDOKU - 12 (Solution)

Kids (6 x 6)

1	3	4	5	2	6
6	5	2	4	3	1
5	2	6	1	4	3
4	1	3	2	6	5
3	4	1	6	5	2
2	6	5	3	1	4

NUMBER PLACE

Number Place is played on a rectangular grid, in which some cells of the grid are shaded. Additionally, external to the grid, several numeric values are given, some denoted as horizontal, and some denoted as vertical.

The puzzle functions as a simple numeric crossword puzzle. The object is to fill in the empty cells with single digits, such that the given numeric values appear on the grid in the orientation specified.

NUMBER PLACE - 1

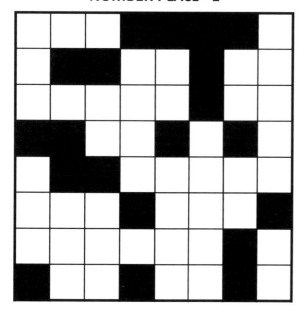

ACROSS

577173,
41, 635, 26,
24, 26717,
62125, 17,
42, 145, 67,
773

DOWN

27337, 12,
572, 75,
64127, 15,
315, 726,
1262, 474,
24, 53,
6676

NUMBER PLACE - 2

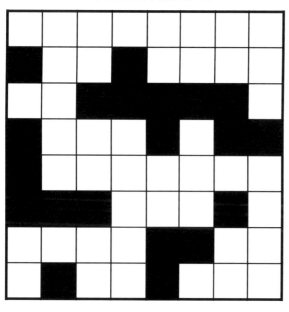

ACROSS

1171, 415,
65, 7236,
7173542,
773, 355,
14, 26, 16,
54136243

DOWN

57764, 51,
2665, 47,
42537, 61,
21, 11, 31,
16, 316, 37,
753, 74

NUMBER PLACE - 3

ACROSS

33, 363, 47126, 746, 41, 4674, 75, 55, 11344361, 73634

DOWN

143, 233, 165, 32, 51744, 43, 473, 4353, 17, 41, 74, 66, 673, 146, 37

NUMBER PLACE - 4

ACROSS

643, 52, 5541, 35, 65, 25, 47657, 77, 76, 55, 6642, 14, 35347, 62

DOWN

74, 77, 623, 247, 63, 56763, 55, 14, 541, 4224656, 635, 54575

NUMBER PLACE - 5

ACROSS

16, 226, 57, 5475651, 623265, 4561, 541, 67, 15717

DOWN

53672, 1642, 14265555, 555, 651, 77164666, 61, 52, 71

NUMBER PLACE - 6

ACROSS

615, 733, 14, 7545244, 667, 761, 46, 12, 732, 4315, 25, 62

DOWN

4611, 461, 27, 62, 46575, 424, 5652365, 657473, 2573

NUMBER PLACE - 1 (Solution)

7	7	3	■	■	■	■	6
2	■	■	1	7	■	2	4
6	2	1	2	5	■	4	1
■	■	2	6	■	2	■	2
3	■	■	2	6	7	1	7
1	4	5	■	6	3	5	■
5	7	7	1	7	3	■	5
■	4	2	■	6	7	■	3

ACROSS

577173, 41, 635, 26, 24, 26717, 62125, 17, 42, 145, 67, 773

DOWN

27337, 12, 572, 75, 64127, 15, 315, 726, 1262, 474, 24, 53, 6676

NUMBER PLACE - 2 (Solution)

5	4	1	3	6	2	4	3
■	2	6	■	1	1	7	1
6	5	■	■	■	■	■	6
■	3	5	5	■	7	■	■
■	7	1	7	3	5	4	2
■	■	7	7	3	■	■	6
7	2	3	6	■	■	1	6
4	■	1	4	■	4	1	5

ACROSS

1171, 415, 65, 7236, 7173542, 773, 355, 14, 26, 16, 54136243

DOWN

57764, 51, 2665, 47, 42537, 61, 21, 11, 31, 16, 316, 37, 753, 74

NUMBER PLACE - 3 (Solution)

4	■	4	7	1	2	6	■
1	1	3	4	4	3	6	1
■	7	5	■	3	3	■	6
3	■	3	■	■	■	5	5
2	■	■	4	1	■	1	■
■	4	6	7	4	■	7	■
4	■	7	3	6	3	4	■
3	6	3	■	■	7	4	6

ACROSS

33, 363, 47126, 746, 41, 4674, 75, 55, 11344361, 73634

DOWN

143, 233, 165, 32, 51744, 43, 473, 4353, 17, 41, 74, 66, 673, 146, 37

NUMBER PLACE - 4 (Solution)

■	■	6	■	5	5	■	5
6	4	3	■	4	■	1	4
■	2	5	■	5	5	4	1
5	2	■	■	7	6	■	■
■	4	7	6	5	7	■	1
6	6	4	2	■	6	2	■
3	5	■	3	5	3	4	7
■	6	5	■	5	■	7	7

ACROSS

643, 52, 5541, 35, 65, 25, 47657, 77, 76, 55, 6642, 14, 35347, 62

DOWN

74, 77, 623, 247, 63, 56763, 55, 14, 541, 4224656, 635, 54575

NUMBER PLACE - 5 (Solution)

ACROSS

16, 226, 57, 5475651, 623265, 4561, 541, 67, 15717

DOWN

53672, 1642, 14265555, 555, 651, 77164666, 61, 52, 71

NUMBER PLACE - 6 (Solution)

ACROSS

615, 733, 14, 7545244, 667, 761, 46, 12, 732, 4315, 25, 62

DOWN

4611, 461, 27, 62, 46575, 424, 5652365, 657473, 2573

SKYSCRAPER

A Skyscraper puzzle consists of a square grid with some exterior 'skyscraper' clues.

Every square in the grid must be filled with a digit from 1 to n (n is the size of the grid) so that every row and column contains one of each digit.

In Skyscraper each digit placed in the grid can be visualised as a building of that many storeys. A '5' is a 5 storey building, for example.

Each number outside the grid reveals the number of 'buildings' that can be seen from that point, looking along the adjacent row or column.

Every building blocks all buildings of a lower height from view, while taller buildings are still visible beyond it.

SKYSCRAPER - 1
Intermediate

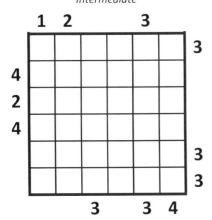

SKYSCRAPER - 2
Intermediate

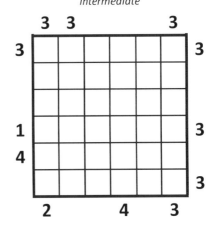

SKYSCRAPER - 3
Intermediate

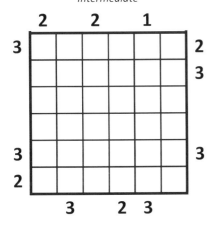

SKYSCRAPER - 4
Intermediate

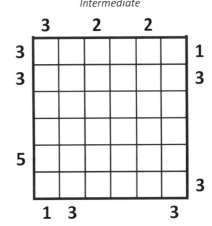

SKYSCRAPER - 5
Intermediate

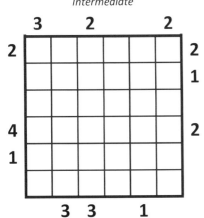

SKYSCRAPER - 6
Intermediate

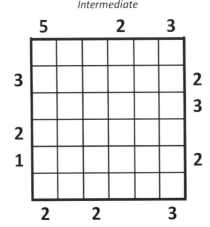

SKYSCRAPER - 7
Intermediate

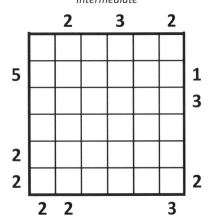

SKYSCRAPER - 8
Intermediate

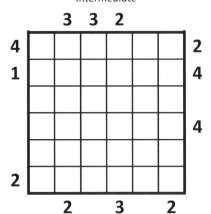

SKYSCRAPER - 9
Intermediate

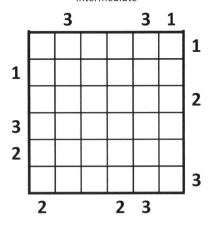

SKYSCRAPER - 10
Intermediate

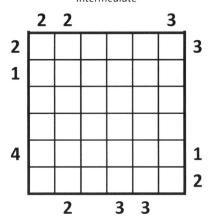

SKYSCRAPER - 11
Intermediate

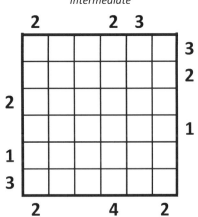

SKYSCRAPER - 12
Intermediate

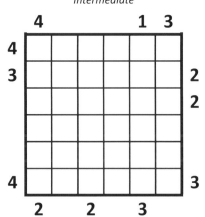

SKYSCRAPER - 13
Intermediate

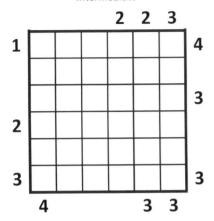

SKYSCRAPER - 14
Intermediate

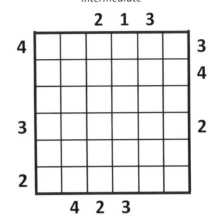

SKYSCRAPER - 15
Intermediate

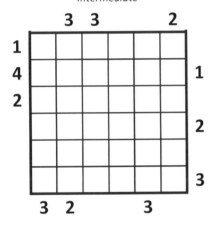

SKYSCRAPER - 16
Intermediate

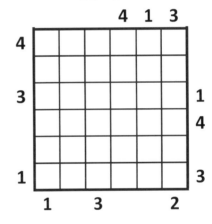

SKYSCRAPER - 17
Intermediate

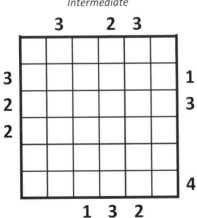

SKYSCRAPER - 18
Intermediate

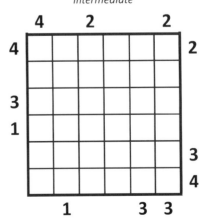

SKYSCRAPER - 1 (Solution)
Intermediate

	1	2	3	5	3	2	
1	6	5	2	1	3	4	3
4	3	1	4	2	5	6	1
2	5	4	6	3	2	1	4
4	2	3	1	4	6	5	2
4	1	2	5	6	4	3	3
2	4	6	3	5	1	2	3
	3	1	3	2	3	4	

SKYSCRAPER - 2 (Solution)
Intermediate

	3	3	1	2	2	3	
3	3	4	6	2	5	1	3
2	5	2	1	6	3	4	2
3	1	5	2	3	4	6	1
1	6	3	4	5	1	2	3
4	2	1	3	4	6	5	2
2	4	6	5	1	2	3	3
	2	1	2	4	2	3	

SKYSCRAPER - 3 (Solution)
Intermediate

	2	2	2	3	1	4	
3	3	2	5	4	6	1	2
2	1	6	4	5	2	3	3
1	6	3	2	1	4	5	2
3	4	5	1	2	3	6	1
3	2	1	3	6	5	4	3
2	5	4	6	3	1	2	3
	2	3	1	2	3	3	

SKYSCRAPER - 4 (Solution)
Intermediate

	3	3	2	3	2	1	
3	4	2	3	1	5	6	1
3	1	5	6	3	4	2	3
2	5	4	1	6	2	3	2
2	3	6	2	4	1	5	2
5	2	3	4	5	6	1	2
1	6	1	5	2	3	4	3
	1	3	2	3	2	3	

SKYSCRAPER - 5 (Solution)
Intermediate

	3	1	2	4	4	2	
2	3	6	4	1	2	5	2
3	1	5	2	3	4	6	1
2	4	1	6	5	3	2	4
4	2	3	5	6	1	4	2
1	6	2	1	4	5	3	3
2	5	4	3	2	6	1	2
	2	3	3	3	1	4	

SKYSCRAPER - 6 (Solution)
Intermediate

	5	3	2	2	1	3	
5	1	3	4	5	6	2	2
3	2	5	6	1	3	4	2
2	4	6	1	2	5	3	3
2	5	2	3	4	1	6	1
1	6	1	2	3	4	5	2
4	3	4	5	6	2	1	3
	2	2	2	1	4	3	

SKYSCRAPER - 7 (Solution)
Intermediate

	1	2	4	3	3	2	
1	6	5	1	3	4	2	4
5	2	3	4	5	1	6	1
2	1	6	5	2	3	4	3
2	4	2	3	6	5	1	3
2	3	1	6	4	2	5	2
2	5	4	2	1	6	3	2
	2	2	2	3	1	3	

SKYSCRAPER - 8 (Solution)
Intermediate

	2	3	3	2	1	2	
4	1	2	4	3	6	5	2
1	6	5	3	2	4	1	4
3	3	4	1	6	5	2	3
2	2	6	5	4	1	3	4
3	4	1	2	5	3	6	1
2	5	3	6	1	2	4	2
	2	2	1	3	4	2	

SKYSCRAPER - 9 (Solution)
Intermediate

	2	3	3	2	3	1	
4	2	1	4	5	3	6	1
1	6	5	3	2	4	1	4
4	1	2	5	3	6	4	2
3	3	4	6	1	2	5	2
2	4	3	1	6	5	2	3
2	5	6	2	4	1	3	3
	2	1	2	2	3	3	

SKYSCRAPER - 10 (Solution)
Intermediate

	2	2	3	1	2	3	
2	4	3	1	6	5	2	3
1	6	2	5	3	4	1	4
4	2	1	3	4	6	5	2
2	5	6	4	1	2	3	3
4	1	4	2	5	3	6	1
3	3	5	6	2	1	4	2
	3	2	1	3	3	2	

SKYSCRAPER - 11 (Solution)
Intermediate

	2	3	1	2	3	3	
2	5	1	6	2	4	3	3
3	3	4	2	6	1	5	2
2	2	6	1	5	3	4	3
3	4	3	5	1	2	6	1
1	6	2	3	4	5	1	3
3	1	5	4	3	6	2	2
	2	2	3	4	1	2	

SKYSCRAPER - 12 (Solution)
Intermediate

	4	3	2	2	1	3	
4	2	3	1	5	6	4	2
3	4	5	6	2	1	3	2
2	3	6	2	1	4	5	2
2	5	1	4	3	2	6	1
1	6	2	3	4	5	1	3
4	1	4	5	6	3	2	3
	2	2	2	1	3	2	

SKYSCRAPER - 13 (Solution)
Intermediate

	1	2	3	2	2	3	
1	6	4	1	5	3	2	4
3	3	2	5	1	6	4	2
2	4	6	2	3	5	1	3
2	5	1	3	4	2	6	1
4	2	3	4	6	1	5	2
3	1	5	6	2	4	3	3
	4	2	1	2	3	3	

SKYSCRAPER - 14 (Solution)
Intermediate

	2	2	2	1	3	5	
4	2	3	5	6	4	1	3
1	6	1	4	5	3	2	4
2	3	6	2	1	5	4	3
3	4	5	1	2	6	3	2
3	1	4	6	3	2	5	2
2	5	2	3	4	1	6	1
	2	4	2	3	3	1	

SKYSCRAPER - 15 (Solution)
Intermediate

	1	3	3	2	2	2	
1	6	3	1	5	2	4	3
4	2	4	5	3	1	6	1
2	5	2	4	1	6	3	2
2	3	1	6	2	4	5	2
2	1	6	3	4	5	2	3
3	4	5	2	6	3	1	3
	3	2	3	1	3	4	

SKYSCRAPER - 16 (Solution)
Intermediate

	6	3	2	4	1	3	
4	1	4	5	3	6	2	2
3	2	3	6	4	1	5	2
3	3	5	1	2	4	6	1
2	4	6	2	5	3	1	4
2	5	1	4	6	2	3	2
1	6	2	3	1	5	4	3
	1	2	3	2	2	2	

SKYSCRAPER - 17 (Solution)
Intermediate

	1	3	3	2	3	2	
1	6	1	2	3	4	5	2
3	4	3	5	2	1	6	1
2	2	6	3	1	5	4	3
2	5	4	1	6	2	3	2
4	3	2	4	5	6	1	2
3	1	5	6	4	3	2	4
	4	2	1	3	2	4	

SKYSCRAPER - 18 (Solution)
Intermediate

	4	3	2	4	1	2	
4	1	3	4	2	6	5	2
3	2	5	6	1	4	3	3
3	4	1	5	3	2	6	1
1	6	2	3	5	1	4	3
3	3	4	2	6	5	1	3
2	5	6	1	4	3	2	4
	2	1	5	2	3	3	

MAZES

The aim is to find your way to the exit after entering the maze. You can use your finger or a pen or pencil to trace your path through the maze.

MAZE - 1

Easy

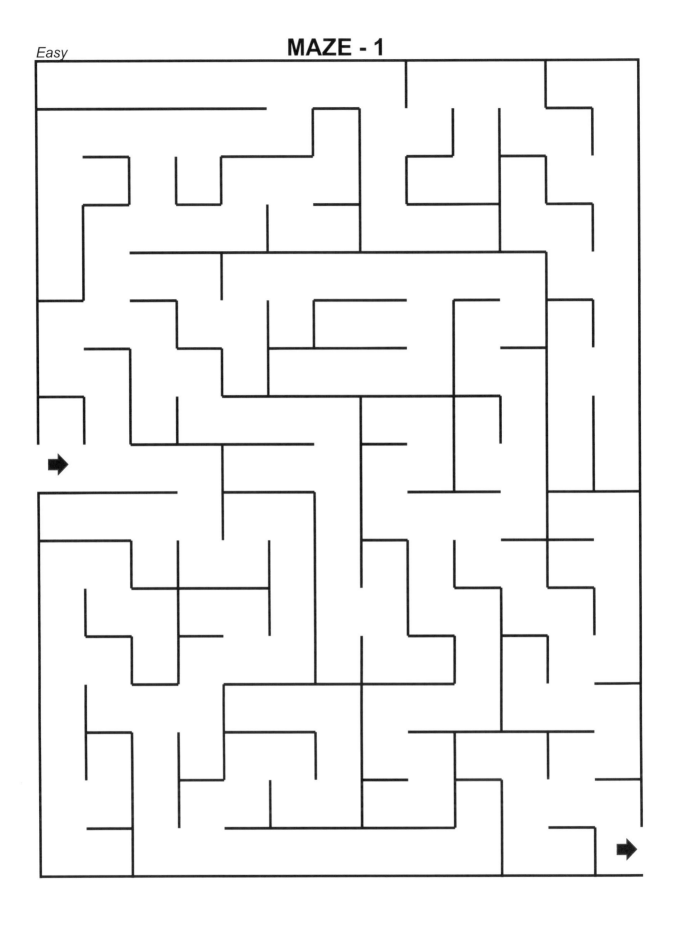

MAZE - 2

Easy

Easy

Easy

MAZE - 2

Easy

MAZE - 3

Easy

WARSHIPS

The only available information are numbers telling you how many ship segments are in each row and column, and some given ship segments in various places in the grid.

The object is to discover where all ten ships are located in the grid.

The fleet consists of
1. battleship (4 squares)
2. cruisers (3 squares)
3. destroyers (2 squares)
4. submarines (1 squares)

A solid block signifies a middle part of a ship.

A curved shape signifies the start or the end of a ship.

The ships may be oriented horizontally and/or vertically in the grid, but not diagonally.

Ships can not occupy adjacent grid squares, even diagonally.

WARSHIPS - 3

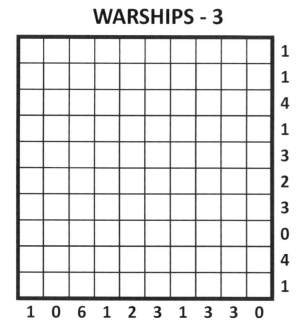

										1
										1
										4
										1
										3
										2
										3
										0
										4
										1
1	0	6	1	2	3	1	3	3	0	

WARSHIPS - 4

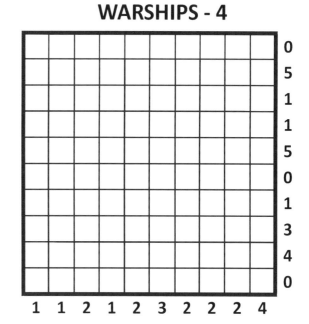

										0
										5
										1
										1
										5
										0
										1
										3
										4
										0
1	1	2	1	2	3	2	2	2	4	

WARSHIPS - 5

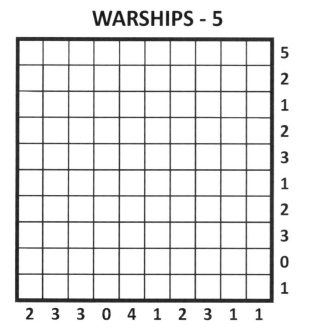

										5
										2
										1
										2
										3
										1
										2
										3
										0
										1
2	3	3	0	4	1	2	3	1	1	

WARSHIPS - 6

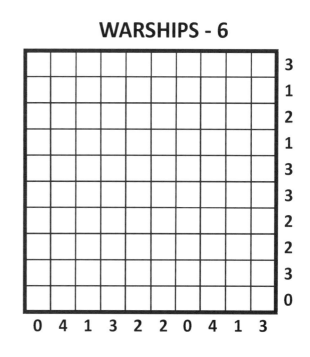

										3
										1
										2
										1
										3
										3
										2
										2
										3
										0
0	4	1	3	2	2	0	4	1	3	

WARSHIPS - 7

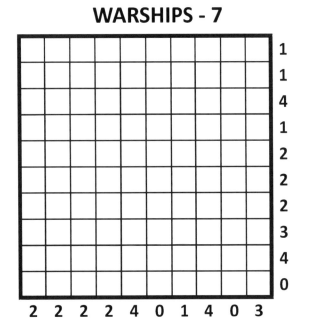

WARSHIPS - 8

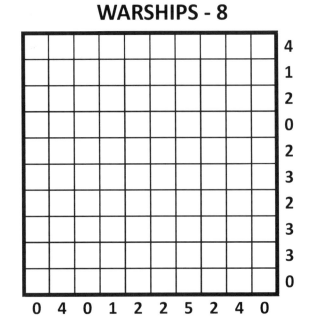

WARSHIPS - 9

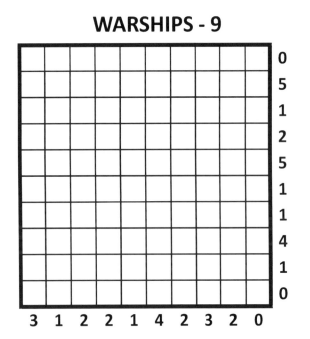

WARSHIPS - 10

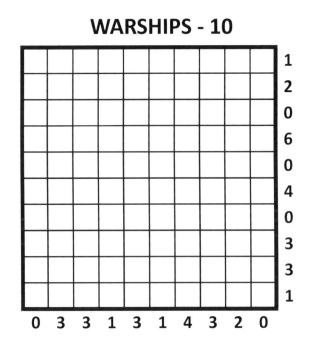

WARSHIPS - 11

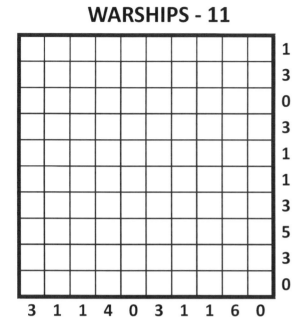

WARSHIPS - 12

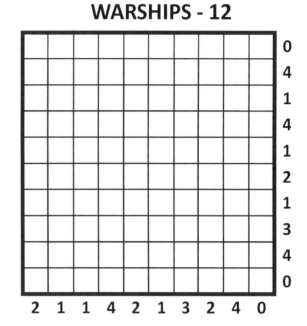

WARSHIPS - 13

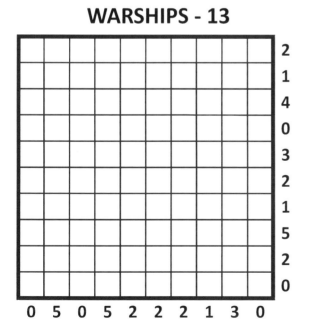

WARSHIPS - 14

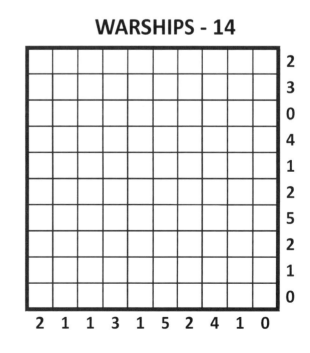

WARSHIPS - 3 (Solution)

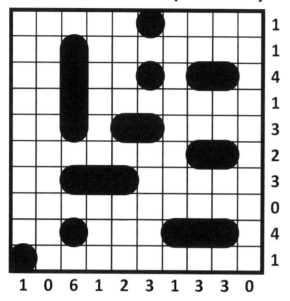

WARSHIPS - 4 (Solution)

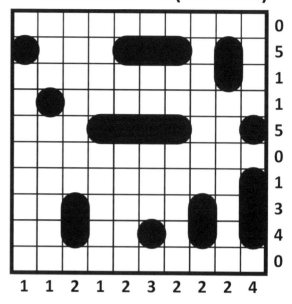

WARSHIPS - 5 (Solution)

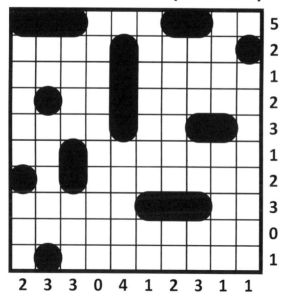

WARSHIPS - 6 (Solution)

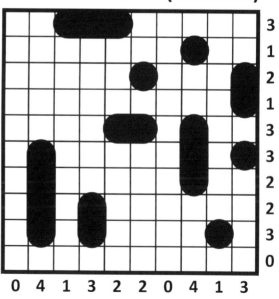

WARSHIPS - 7 (Solution)

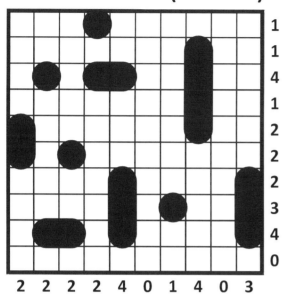

WARSHIPS - 8 (Solution)

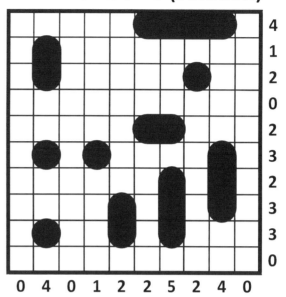

WARSHIPS - 9 (Solution)

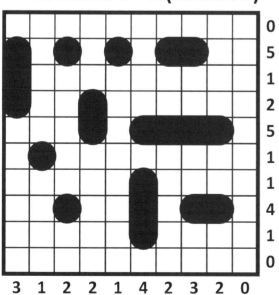

WARSHIPS - 10 (Solution)

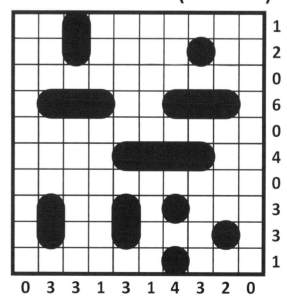

WARSHIPS - 11 (Solution)

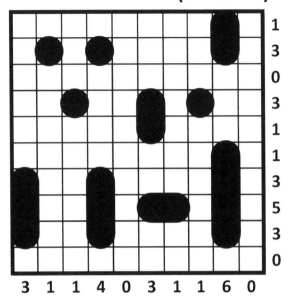

WARSHIPS - 12 (Solution)

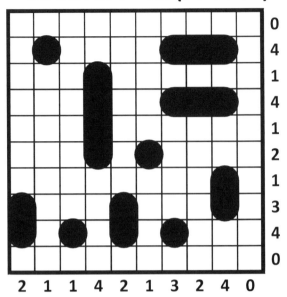

WARSHIPS - 13 (Solution)

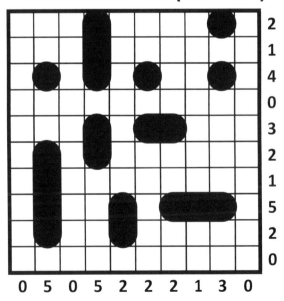

WARSHIPS - 14 (Solution)

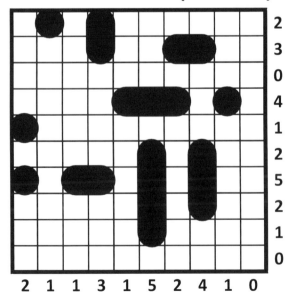

WORD SCRAMBLE

The aim is to find as many words as you can in the grid within 4 minutes, whilst adhering to the following rules

-The letters must be adjoining in a 'chain'. (Letters in the chain may be adjacent horizontally, vertically, or diagonally.)
-Each word must contain at least three letters.
-No letter 'box' may be used more than once within a single word.

SCORING

The scoring is as follow

Fewer than 3 Letters no score
3 Letters 1 point
4 Letters 1 point
5 Letters 2 points
6 Letters 3 points
7 Letters 4 points
8 or More Letters 11 points

RULES

-You can mark down the singular and plural forms of a noun e.g. dog & dogs
- You may only write a word down once even if you can form it with different letter 'boxes'
- Any word that is found in the Dictionary is allowed
- You can mark down words within other words e.g. with angled you could also have led and angle

Puzzle #21
WOMEN EMPOWERMENT

FNEMENII

EBAB

ORHN

ERLTKI

BEOTOE

HLCTCU

CHOMA

IOSMNSYMGI

DERUTS

AFGTSISUFR

GFEUER

ENIEILRG

Puzzle #22
WINTER

YNWEOHDE   ☐☐☐☐☐☐☐☐

EYRPZH   ☐☐☐☐☐☐

EWNTRTEMII   ☐☐☐☐☐☐☐☐☐☐

RLBHAINE   ☐☐☐☐☐☐☐☐

NONETYE   ☐☐☐☐☐☐☐

HEIWT   ☐☐☐☐☐

DAONSI   ☐☐☐☐☐☐

REAVOOCT   ☐☐☐☐☐☐☐☐

OSTER   ☐☐☐☐☐

ICORM   ☐☐☐☐☐

MRFO   ☐☐☐☐

ELACURUXNI   ☐☐☐☐☐☐☐☐☐☐

WOMEN EMPOWERMENT

FNEMENII	=	FEMININE
EBAB	=	BABE
ORHN	=	HORN
ERLTKI	=	KIRTLE
BEOTOE	=	BOOTEE
HLCTCU	=	CLUTCH
CHOMA	=	MACHO
IOSMNSYMGI	=	MISOGYNISM
DERUTS	=	DUSTER
AFGTSISUFR	=	SUFFRAGIST
GFEUER	=	REFUGE
ENIEILRG	=	LINGERIE

WINTER

YNWEOHDE	=	HONEYDEW
EYRPZH	=	ZEPHYR
EWNTRTEMII	=	WINTERTIME
RLBHAINE	=	HIBERNAL
NONETYE	=	NEOTENY
HEIWT	=	WHITE
DAONSI	=	ADONIS
REAVOOCT	=	OVERCOAT
OSTER	=	STORE
ICORM	=	MICRO
MRFO	=	FORM
ELACURUXNI	=	LUXURIANCE

CALCUDOKU

Each puzzle consists of a grid containing blocks surrounded by bold lines. The object is to fill all empty squares so that the numbers 1 to N (where N is the number of rows or columns in the grid) appear exactly once in each row and column and the numbers in each block produce the result shown in the top-left corner of the block according to the math operation appearing on the top of the grid. In CalcuDoku a number may be used more than once in the same block. Single, double or multi-operator can be used.

In multi-operator option, all operators could not be used in a grid.

CALCUDOKU - 1

4÷				60x
	12x	2÷		
	20x		6x	
		3÷		
9+	3	5x		12+

CALCUDOKU - 2

		4		
12+		9+		200x
	12+		24x	3
	2-			1

CALCUDOKU - 3

3	5		2÷	12+
			24x	
	2÷			
	4		2-	
	30x	12+		

CALCUDOKU - 4

				12x
	30x		2÷	5
1-			1-	2
1÷		2		
	2÷	60x		

CALCUDOKU - 5

3	4		3-	10+
			12x	
	7+			
	5	1-		
	20x	12+		

CALCUDOKU - 6

	2÷		1-	
		1-		36x
20x	5÷			
	4			50x
5+	3		4÷	

CALCUDOKU - 7

	9+	1-		1
5+				3-
1	6x			
	40x		5÷	
		1-	3	9+

CALCUDOKU - 8

	3÷		2÷	
		7+		30x
20x	3-			
	4			30x
1-	5		4÷	

CALCUDOKU - 9

			50x	
	12x		9+	
5	2	6+		
120x		4÷		1-
			3÷	

CALCUDOKU - 10

	1-		2-	
		3-		30x
24x	4÷			
	2			60x
5÷	3		2÷	

CALCUDOKU - 11

		4	5	
13+		20x	1÷	
	7+		1-	
	15x			1-
		1÷		

CALCUDOKU - 12

10x			3x	
4÷				4÷
	15x	24x		14+
10+		5x		
			10x	

CALCUDOKU - 1 (Solution)

4÷ 1	4	2	5	60x 3
3	12x 2	2÷ 1	4	5
2	20x 5	4	6x 3	1
5	1	3÷ 3	2	4
9+ 4	3 3	5x 5	1	12+ 2

CALCUDOKU - 2 (Solution)

3	1	4 4	2	5
12+ 1	2	9+ 3	5	200x 4
2	12+ 4	5	24x 1	3 3
4	2- 5	2	3	1 1
5	3	1	4	2

CALCUDOKU - 3 (Solution)

3 3	5 5	1	2÷ 2	12+ 4
4	1	2	24x 3	5
5	2÷ 2	4	1	3
1	4 4	3	2- 5	2
2	30x 3	12+ 5	4	1

CALCUDOKU - 4 (Solution)

5	2	4	1	12x 3
4	30x 3	1	2÷ 2	5 5
1- 3	1	5	1- 4	2 2
1÷ 1	5	2 2	3	4
2	2÷ 4	60x 3	5	1

CALCUDOKU - 5 (Solution)

3 [3]	4 [4]	2	5 [3-]	1 [10+]
2	3	4	1 [12x]	5
5	2 [7+]	1	3	4
1	5 [5]	3	4 [1-]	2
4	1 [20x]	5 [12+]	2	3

CALCUDOKU - 6 (Solution)

1	2 [2÷]	3	4 [1-]	5
5	1	4 [1-]	2	3 [36x]
4 [20x]	5 [5÷]	1	3	2
3	4 [4]	2	5	1 [50x]
2 [5+]	3 [3]	5	1 [4÷]	4

CALCUDOKU - 7 (Solution)

2	5 [9+]	3 [1-]	4	1 [1]
3 [5+]	4	1	2	5 [3-]
1 [1]	3 [6x]	2	5	4
4	2 [40x]	5	1 [5÷]	3
5	1	4 [1-]	3 [3]	2 [9+]

CALCUDOKU - 8 (Solution)

5	1 [3÷]	3	4 [2÷]	2
1	3	4 [7+]	2	5 [30x]
4 [20x]	2 [3-]	5	3	1
2	4 [4]	1	5	3 [30x]
3 [1-]	5 [5]	2	1 [4÷]	4

CALCUDOKU - 9 (Solution)

4	1	2	50x 5	3
1	12x 3	5	9+ 4	2
5 5	2 2	6+ 3	1	4
120x 3	4	4÷ 1	2	1- 5
2	5	4	3÷ 3	1

CALCUDOKU - 10 (Solution)

4	1- 5	2	2- 1	3
3	4	3- 5	2	30x 1
24x 2	4÷ 1	4	3	5
1	2 2	3	5	60x 4
5÷ 5	3 3	1	2÷ 4	2

CALCUDOKU - 11 (Solution)

2	1	4 4	5 5	3
13+ 4	2	20x 5	1÷ 3	1
5	7+ 4	3	1- 1	2
1	15x 3	2	4	1- 5
3	5	1÷ 1	2	4

CALCUDOKU - 12 (Solution)

10x 5	2	3	3x 1	4
4÷ 4	5	2	3	4÷ 1
1	15x 3	24x 4	2	14+ 5
10+ 2	1	5x 5	4	3
3	4	1	10x 5	2

TIC- TAC-LOGIC

Tic-Tac-Logic is a single player puzzle based on tic-tac-toe.
Each puzzle consists of a grid containing X's and O's in various places.

The object is to place X or O in the remaining squares so that
1. there are no more than two consecutive X's or O's in a row or column;
2. the number of X's is the same as the number of O's in each row and column; and
3. all rows and all columns are unique.

TIC TAC LOGIC - 1

	X		X		O
		O	O		
X		X			X
	O			O	O
O		O		X	
	O		O		X

TIC TAC LOGIC - 2

O		X		X	O
	X	O		X	
			X		X
O	X				
	O	O		X	O
O		X		O	

TIC TAC LOGIC - 3

X		O		O	
	O		X	O	
X		O			O
	X			O	
O		X		X	X
	X	X			O

TIC TAC LOGIC - 4

O			O	O	
	X			X	O
O		X	X		
O	X				X
		X		O	O
X		O		X	

TIC TAC LOGIC - 5

	X		O		O
X		O		O	
O		X		O	X
			O		
X	X		O		O
	O	O		O	

TIC TAC LOGIC - 6

	X			X	O
X		O	O		
		O			X
	X			O	
X		O	X		O
	O		X	O	

TIC TAC LOGIC - 7

O		O		O	
	O		X		
	X	X		X	O
O			O	X	
	O	X			
X		X			O

TIC TAC LOGIC - 8

	O	O		O	
O	O		O		X
		O			O
	X		O	X	
O	O			O	X
O		X			

TIC TAC LOGIC - 9

O		X		X	
	O	X			O
O	X		O		
				O	
	X	O			O
X		O	O		

TIC TAC LOGIC - 10

X			O		O
	O		X		X
	X	X		X	
X		O		X	O
	X				
X	O		X		X

TIC TAC LOGIC - 11

X		X		X	
	X		O		O
	X		X		
X				X	O
	X	X			X
X			O		O

TIC TAC LOGIC - 12

	X	X		O	
X	X		X		
X		X			O
	X		X		X
	O		O	X	
X		O		X	

TIC TAC LOGIC - 1 (Solution)

X	X	O	X	O	O
O	X	O	O	X	X
X	O	X	O	O	X
X	O	X	X	O	O
O	X	O	X	X	O
O	O	X	O	X	X

TIC TAC LOGIC - 2 (Solution)

O	X	X	O	X	O
X	X	O	O	X	O
X	O	O	X	O	X
O	X	X	O	O	X
X	O	O	X	X	O
O	O	X	X	O	X

TIC TAC LOGIC - 3 (Solution)

X	O	O	X	O	X
O	O	X	X	O	X
X	X	O	O	X	O
X	X	O	X	O	O
O	O	X	O	X	X
O	X	X	O	X	O

TIC TAC LOGIC - 4 (Solution)

O	X	X	O	O	X
X	X	O	O	X	O
O	O	X	X	O	X
O	X	O	O	X	X
X	O	X	X	O	O
X	O	O	X	X	O

TIC TAC LOGIC - 5 (Solution)

O	X	X	O	X	O
X	X	O	X	O	O
O	O	X	X	O	X
O	O	X	O	X	X
X	X	O	O	X	O
X	O	O	X	O	X

TIC TAC LOGIC - 6 (Solution)

O	X	X	O	X	O
X	X	O	O	X	O
X	O	O	X	O	X
O	X	X	O	O	X
X	O	O	X	X	O
O	O	X	X	O	X

TIC TAC LOGIC - 7 (Solution)

O	X	O	X	O	X
X	O	O	X	O	X
O	X	X	O	X	O
O	X	O	O	X	X
X	O	X	X	O	O
X	O	X	O	X	O

TIC TAC LOGIC - 8 (Solution)

X	O	O	X	O	X
O	O	X	O	X	X
X	X	O	X	O	O
X	X	O	O	X	O
O	O	X	X	O	X
O	X	X	O	X	O

TIC TAC LOGIC - 9 (Solution)

O	O	X	O	X	X
X	O	X	X	O	O
O	X	O	O	X	X
O	O	X	X	O	X
X	X	O	X	O	O
X	X	O	O	X	O

TIC TAC LOGIC - 10 (Solution)

X	X	O	O	X	O
O	O	X	X	O	X
O	X	X	O	X	O
X	O	O	X	X	O
O	X	X	O	O	X
X	O	O	X	O	X

TIC TAC LOGIC - 11 (Solution)

X	O	X	O	X	O
O	X	X	O	X	O
O	X	O	X	O	X
X	O	O	X	X	O
O	X	X	O	O	X
X	O	O	X	O	X

TIC TAC LOGIC - 12 (Solution)

O	X	X	O	O	X
X	X	O	X	O	O
X	O	X	O	X	O
O	X	O	X	O	X
O	O	X	O	X	X
X	O	O	X	X	O

MINES FINDER

There are a series of mines hidden randomly in the grid. You need to work out the location of these mines and mark them in.

To help you work out the location of the mines some squares have a number in. This number tells you the number of mines
that are hidden in adjacent squares to that one, up, down, left, right and diagonal.

Squares that contain a numbers cannot contain a mine.

MINES FINDER - 1

1	3			
2				
3		7		
	4			
2		3	3	2

MINES FINDER - 2

2	4			3
	8		6	3
				1
3			3	1

MINES FINDER - 3

2				3
	7			
				3
2	5		5	2
	2			1

MINES FINDER - 4

3				2
				2
5			5	2
				1
	5		3	1

MINES FINDER - 5

2			2	1
4		7		3
5				3
			3	1

MINES FINDER - 6

2		5		3
4				
3	5			3
1		3	2	1

MINES FINDER - 7

2			2	
3			4	2
4		7		
	5			3

MINES FINDER - 8

2		4	4	
4				
4		7		3
2			2	1

MINES FINDER - 9

2	4		3	1
				3
4				
	6			4
		4		2

MINES FINDER - 10

3			4	2
		6		4
3	5		5	
	3			2

MINES FINDER - 11

2		5		2
4				3
				3
		7		4
3		4		

MINES FINDER - 12

2			2	
4			5	2
3	5			
1		4		

MINES FINDER - 1 (Solution)

1	3	●	●	●
2	●	●	●	●
3	●	7	●	●
●	4	●	●	●
2	●	3	3	2

MINES FINDER - 2 (Solution)

2	4	●	●	3
●	●	●	●	●
●	8	●	6	3
●	●	●	●	1
3	●	●	3	1

MINES FINDER - 3 (Solution)

2	●	●	●	3
●	7	●	●	●
●	●	●	●	3
2	5	●	5	2
	2	●	●	1

MINES FINDER - 4 (Solution)

3	●	●	●	2
●	●	●	●	2
5	●	●	5	2
●	●	●	●	1
●	5	●	3	1

MINES FINDER - 5 (Solution)

2	●	●	2	1
4	●	7	●	3
●	●	●	●	●
5	●	●	●	3
●	●	●	3	1

MINES FINDER - 6 (Solution)

2	●	5	●	3
4	●	●	●	●
●	●	●	●	●
3	5	●	●	3
1	●	3	2	1

MINES FINDER - 7 (Solution)

2	●	●	2	
3	●	●	4	2
4	●	7	●	●
●	●	●	●	●
●	5	●	●	3

MINES FINDER - 8 (Solution)

2	●	4	4	●
4	●	●	●	●
●	●	●	●	●
4	●	7	●	3
2	●	●	2	1

MINES FINDER - 9 (Solution)

2	4	●	3	1
●	●	●	●	3
4	●	●	●	●
●	6	●	●	4
●	●	4	●	2

MINES FINDER - 10

3	●	●	4	2
●	●	●	●	●
●	●	6	●	4
3	5	●	5	●
●	3	●	●	2

MINES FINDER - 11

2	●	5	●	2
4	●	●	●	3
●	●	●	●	3
●	●	7	●	4
3	●	4	●	●

MINES FINDER - 12

2	●	●	2	
4	●	●	5	2
●	●	●	●	●
3	5	●	●	●
1	●	4	●	●

CROSSWORD

A crossword is a word puzzle that usually takes the form of a square or a rectangular grid of white- and black-shaded squares.

The game's goal is to fill the white squares with letters, forming words or phrases, by solving clues, which lead to the answers.

In languages that are written left-to-right, the answer words and phrases are placed in the grid from left to right ("Across") and from top to bottom ("Down").

The shaded squares are used to separate the words or phrases.

CROSSWORD Puzzle : 15

ACROSS

1. Not kosher
5. Slur over
10. Is not
14. Dry riverbed
15. Delicatessens
16. Hitler's autobiography, "- Kampf"
17. Notion
18. Excrete
19. Germinated grain
20. Biblical strongman
22. Vinegary
24. Region
25. Polyp colony
26. Lubricates
29. Fats
33. Jump
36. Act of heating
40. Lazy
42. Merrier
43. Dame - Everage, Humphries' character
44. Exist together
47. Extrasensory perception
48. Sauerkraut
49. Indian pulses
51. Rows
55. Fruit pips
59. Exterior
61. Young swan
62. The Pentateuch
63. Guilt
65. Hereditary factor
66. Islamic call to prayer
67. Applause
68. Islamic chieftain
69. Weal
70. Relaxes
71. Curse

DOWN

1. Distort
2. Navigational aid
3. Dropsy
4. Ignominious failure
5. Paradise
6. Limb
7. Pertaining to the ileum
8. Discotheque
9. Chemical compound
10. Destroy by fire
11. Oceans
12. African river
13. An explosive
21. Auricular
23. Fine powder
27. Delays
28. Lath
30. Travel on
31. Puts on
32. Break suddenly
33. Rube
34. Scent
35. Prayer
37. Optic organ
38. Ward off
39. Curved entrance
41. Triumphant
45. Inflammation (Suffix)
46. Simple
50. Having legs
52. More pleasant
53. Draw forth
54. Vends
56. Purgative injection
57. Jeans fabric
58. Severe
59. Seep
60. European mountain range
61. Felines
62. Choice marble
64. Dab

CROSSWORD Puzzle : 16

ACROSS

1. Marine hazard
5. Manila hemp plant
10. Public swimming pool
14. Australian super-model
15. Citrus fruit
16. Second-hand
17. Let sink
18. Decorate
19. Dressed
20. Underclothes
22. Not asked
24. Paradises
25. Oxidised
26. Supplements
29. Farewell
33. Exclamation of surprise
36. North American birch
40. Let fall
42. Climbing vine
43. Middle Eastern bread
44. Lacks esteem
47. Uncle -, USA personified
48. The Devil
49. Engrave with acid
51. Managed
55. Major artery
59. Outlast
61. Pledge
62. Spanish words of agreement (2.2)
63. Great fear
65. Plot of ground
66. Smart - , show-off
67. Winged
68. Telescope part
69. Wheel cover
70. Harp-like instruments
71. Nervous

DOWN

1. Theatrical parody
2. African antelope
3. Slur over
4. Catlike
5. Woe is me
6. Cot
7. Love affair
8. Horn-shaped bone
9. Indian currency
10. Fundraising game where one takes a chance selecting unknown prizes (5.3)
11. Small island
12. Deceased
13. Rum
21. Portable ice-box
23. Pierce with knife
27. Long fish
28. Slide
30. Eye part
31. Prefix, eight
32. Bogus
33. Appends
34. Opera solo
35. Party holder
37. New Guinea seaport
38. At one time
39. Power unit
41. Custom
45. Enough
46. Confidence trick
50. Tether
52. Foot lever
53. In good time
54. Dismal
56. Breathed rattlingly
57. Nasal tone
58. Restless
59. Greasy
60. Consumer
61. Roman dates
62. Took a seat
64. Dined

CROSSWORD Puzzle : 15

T	R	E	F	■	E	L	I	D	E	■	I	S	N	T
W	A	D	I	■	D	E	L	I	S	■	M	E	I	N
I	D	E	A	■	E	G	E	S	T	■	M	A	L	T
S	A	M	S	O	N	■	A	C	E	T	O	S	E	■
T	R	A	C	T	■	C	O	R	A	L	■	■	■	■
■	■	O	I	L	S	■	■	■	L	A	R	D	S	
H	O	P	■	C	A	L	E	F	A	C	T	I	O	N
I	D	L	E	■	G	A	Y	E	R	■	E	D	N	A
C	O	E	X	I	S	T	E	N	C	E	■	E	S	P
K	R	A	U	T	■	■	D	H	A	L	■	■	■	
■	■	L	I	N	E	S	■	S	E	E	D	S		
■	O	U	T	S	I	D	E	■	C	Y	G	N	E	T
T	O	R	A	■	C	U	L	P	A	■	G	E	N	E
A	Z	A	N	■	E	C	L	A	T	■	E	M	I	R
W	E	L	T	■	R	E	S	T	S	■	D	A	M	N

CROSSWORD Puzzle : 16

R	E	E	F	■	A	B	A	C	A	■	L	I	D	O
E	L	L	E	■	L	E	M	O	N	■	U	S	E	D
V	A	I	L	■	A	D	O	R	N	■	C	L	A	D
U	N	D	I	E	S	■	U	N	A	S	K	E	D	■
E	D	E	N	S	■	■	R	U	S	T	Y	■	■	■
■	■	■	E	K	E	S	■	■	A	D	I	O	S	■
A	A	H	■	Y	E	L	L	O	W	B	I	R	C	H
D	R	O	P	■	L	I	A	N	A	■	P	I	T	A
D	I	S	R	E	S	P	E	C	T	S	■	S	A	M
S	A	T	A	N	■	■	■	E	T	C	H	■	■	■
■	■	■	C	O	P	E	D	■	■	A	O	R	T	A
■	O	U	T	W	E	A	R	■	I	M	P	A	W	N
S	I	S	I	■	D	R	E	A	D	■	P	L	A	T
A	L	E	C	■	A	L	A	T	E	■	L	E	N	S
T	Y	R	E	■	L	Y	R	E	S	■	E	D	G	Y

KRISS
KROSS

N° 1

mots de 4 lettres
Cash
Soph
Tent
Wars

mots de 5 lettres
Hilum
Oxter
Ratch

mots de 6 lettres
Acacia
Afresh
Lose it

mots de 8 lettres
Amoretto
Four-eyes
Loony bin

mots de 10 lettres
Laparotomy
Treble clef

mots de 13 lettres
Matriculating
Rite of passage

mot de 14 lettre
Chelsea tractor

mots de 15 lettres
As a matter of fact
Whole wheat
bread

N° 2

mots de 4 lettres
Pate
Suck

mots de 5 lettres
Didn't
Furry
Indri
Mulct

mots de 7 lettres
Chrisom
Sorrows

mots de 8 lettres
Escaping
Name tags
Pyramids

mot de 9 lettre
Decertify

mots de 10 lettres
Effeminacy
Welsh corgi

mot de 11 lettre
Recommenced

mots de 13 lettres
Nostalgically
Physiotherapy

mots de 15 lettres
Domestic animals
French Polynesia

N° 3

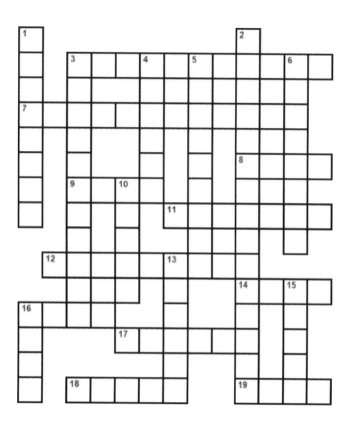

mots de 4 lettres
Dago
Duly
Romp
Taws
Vamp
Yuck

mots de 5 lettres
Medic
Melds
Ogham

mots de 6 lettres
Encamp
Ice cap
Redeem

mot de 7 lettre
Parlays

mots de 8 lettres
Gangways
Son-in-law

mots de 9 lettres
Cheap-jack
Powder keg

mots de 11 lettres
Cod-liver oil
Cover charge

mot de 12 lettre
Indiscretion

mot de 15 lettre
Radiotelegraphy

N° 4

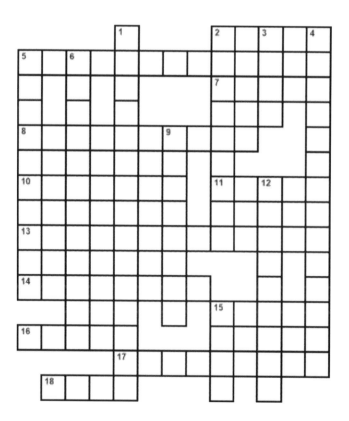

mots de 4 lettres
Aloe
Cups
Phiz

mots de 5 lettres
Chant
Pedro
Quota
Snobs
Tatar

mot de 7 lettre
Wedlock

mots de 8 lettres
Run short
Take part

mots de 9 lettres

Bastinado
Coquettes
Emaciates
Turbidity

mots de 10 lettres
Altogether
Breakwater

mot de 12 lettre
Santo Domingo

mot de 13 lettre
Time exposures

mot de 14 lettre
Transgressions

mot de 15 lettre
Wild-goose chases

N° 1

```
A C A C I A       W A R S
  A H   S O P H   A
  S E A     O X T E R
  H I L U M   L   C   I
    S   A F R E S H   T
L O S E I T     W     E
A     A   T     H     O
P     T R E B L E C L E F
A     R   R   A   O   P
R   A M O R E T T O   A
O   C   F   B   N   S
T E N T   F O U R E Y E S
O     O     A   E   B   A
M A T R I C U L A T I N G
Y     T     D   N   E
```

N° 2

```
      D E C E R T I F Y
        O       E   R
E F F E M I N A C Y   E
  S   U E     A   O   N
C H R I S O M   M U L C T
A   R   T     E   M     H
P H Y S I O T H E R A P Y
I   I   C     A   N     O
N O S T A L G I C A L L Y
G   O   N   S   E   Y
    R   I       D I D N T
P Y R A M I D S   N   E
A   O   A     U   D   S
T   W E L S H C O R G I A
E   S   S     K   I   A
```

N° 3

```
S                 R
O   C O V E R C H A R G E
N   O     N   H   D   A
I N D I S C R E T I O N
N   L     A   A   O   G
L   I     M   P   T A W S
A   V A M P   J   E   A
W   E     E   P A R L A Y S
    R     L   C   E   S
  P O W D E R K E G
    I     S   E   R O M P
D U L Y   D   A   E
A         E   R O M P
G     I C E C A P   D I
O   O G H A M   Y U C K
```

N° 4

```
          W       C H A N T
B A S T I N A D O   L     R
R     A   L       Q U O T A
E     N   D       U   E   N
A L T O G E T H E R   T   S
K   O   O   A     T       G
W E D L O C K   T A T A R
A   O   S   E     E   U   E
T I M E E X P O S U R E S
E   I   C   A     B     S
R U N S H O R T   I     I
      G   A   T P E D R O
S N O B S   H   I   I   N
      E M A C I A T E S
  C U P S   Z   Y
```

NURIKABE

Each puzzle consists of a grid containing clues in various places. The object is to create islands by partitioning between clues with walls so

- Each island contains exactly one clue.
- The number of squares in each island equals the value of the clue.
- All islands are isolated from each other horizontally and vertically.
- There are no wall areas of 2x2 or larger.
- When completed, all walls form a continuous path.

NURIKABE - 1

1					1
		3		2	
	2				
			2		
					1

NURIKABE - 2

1					
	2				
4					6
			5		

NURIKABE - 3

	4				1
		2			
				3	
	2				
1				2	

NURIKABE - 4

	2				
		3		5	6

NURIKABE - 5

1				14	
	2		3		

NURIKABE - 6

1				14	
	2		3		

NURIKABE - 7

	2				
				3	
				1	
				7	

NURIKABE - 8

		10			
			1		
	2				
4					
				2	

NURIKABE - 9

	2				1
				2	
	3				
			2		
1				4	

NURIKABE - 10

6		5		3	
				2	

NURIKABE - 11

				6	
		3			
2					
				2	
					1

NURIKABE - 12

1					
	2				4
				2	
	8				

NURIKABE - 1 (Solution)

NURIKABE - 2 (Solution)

NURIKABE - 3 (Solution)

NURIKABE - 4 (Solution)

NURIKABE - 5 (Solution)

NURIKABE - 6 (Solution)

NURIKABE - 7 (Solution)

NURIKABE - 8 (Solution)

NURIKABE - 9 (Solution)

NURIKABE - 10 (Solution)

NURIKABE - 11 (Solution)

NURIKABE - 12 (Solution)

FUTOSHIKI

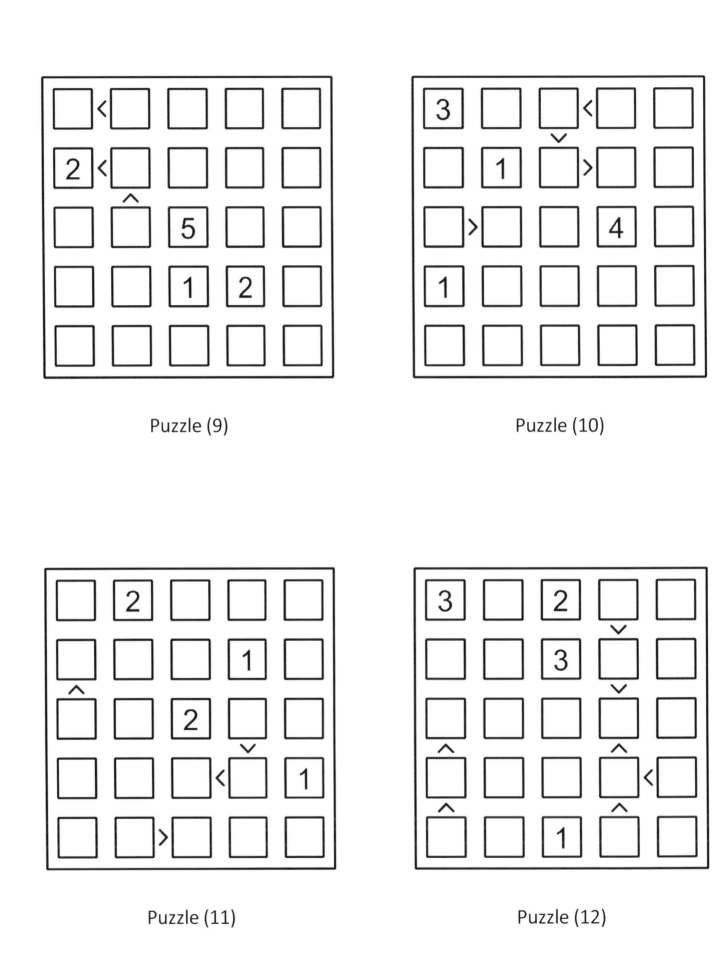

Puzzle (9)

Puzzle (10)

Puzzle (11)

Puzzle (12)

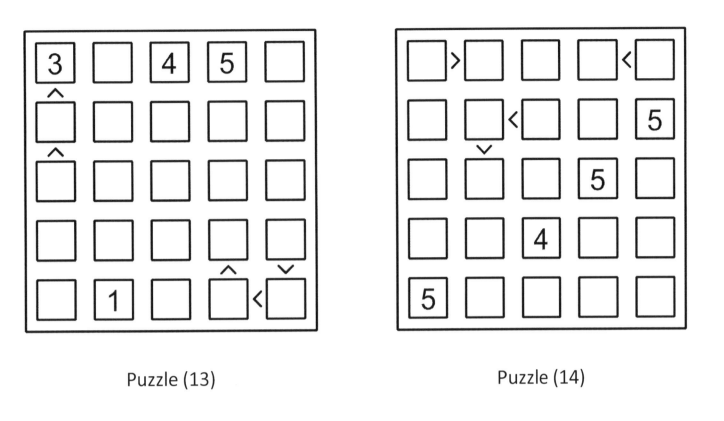

Puzzle (13)   Puzzle (14)

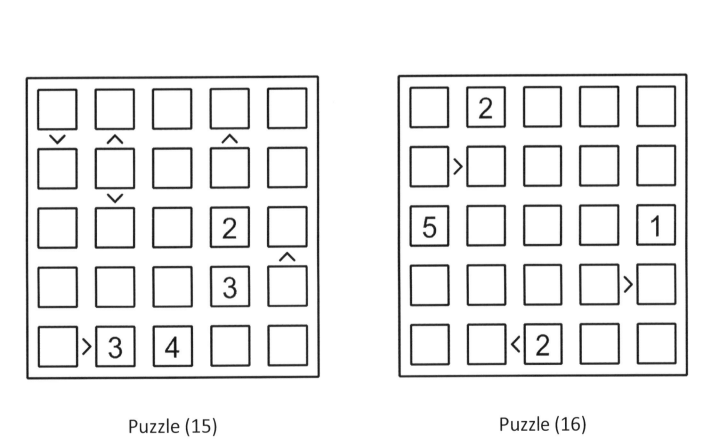

Puzzle (15)   Puzzle (16)

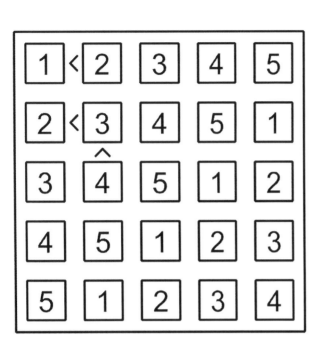

Solution (9)

Solution (10)

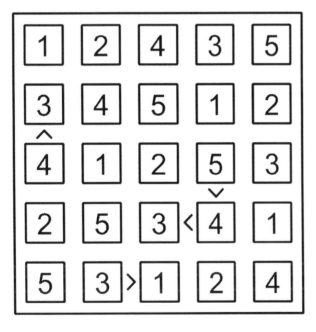

Solution (11)

Solution (12)

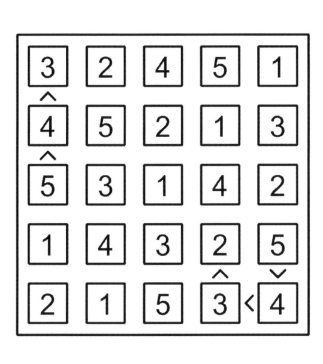

Solution (13)

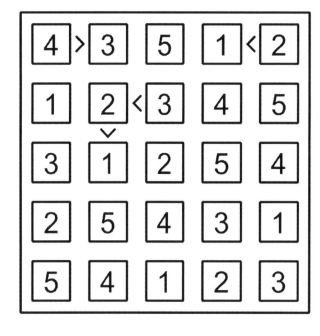

Solution (14)

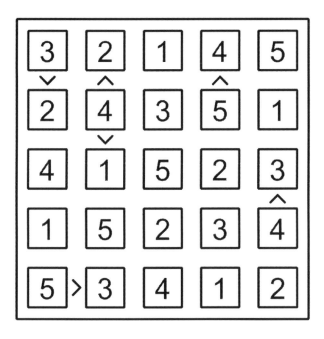

Solution (15)

Solution (16)

KAKURASU

The goal is to fill (color) some cells to satisfy the clues.

The numbers across the bottom and down the right are the clues, and equal the row and column totals for the colored cells.

The numbers across the top and down the left are the values for each of the cells in the rows and columns (the first cell in a row or column is worth 1, the second 2, the third 3, etc.).

KAKURASU - 3

	1	2	3	4	5	
1						3
2						2
3						5
4						11
5						8
	8	11	1	7	9	

KAKURASU - 4

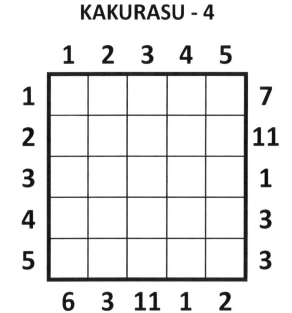

	1	2	3	4	5	
1						7
2						11
3						1
4						3
5						3
	6	3	11	1	2	

KAKURASU - 5

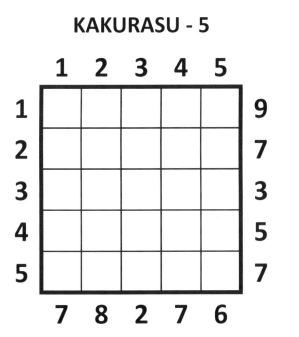

	1	2	3	4	5	
1						9
2						7
3						3
4						5
5						7
	7	8	2	7	6	

KAKURASU - 6

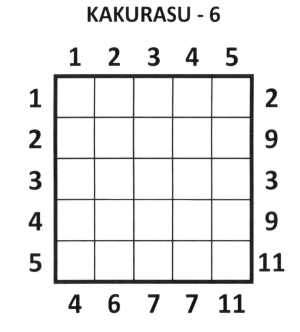

	1	2	3	4	5	
1						2
2						9
3						3
4						9
5						11
	4	6	7	7	11	

KAKURASU - 7

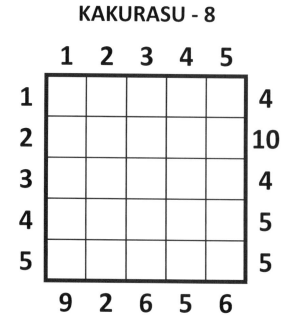

	1	2	3	4	5	
1						5
2						10
3						5
4						6
5						3
	9	4	9	5	3	

KAKURASU - 8

	1	2	3	4	5	
1						4
2						10
3						4
4						5
5						5
	9	2	6	5	6	

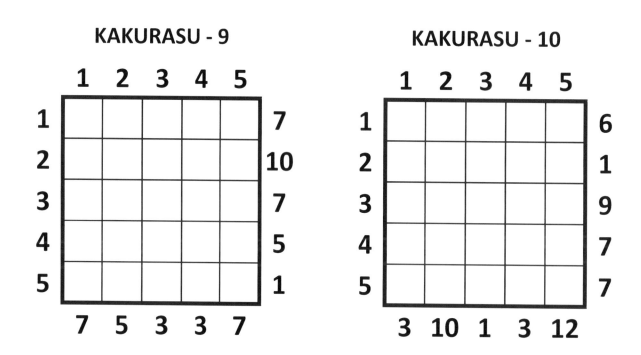

KAKURASU - 9

	1	2	3	4	5	
1						7
2						10
3						7
4						5
5						1
	7	5	3	3	7	

KAKURASU - 10

	1	2	3	4	5	
1						6
2						1
3						9
4						7
5						7
	3	10	1	3	12	

KAKURASU - 11

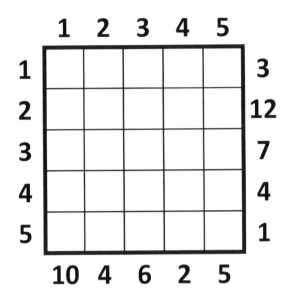

KAKURASU - 12

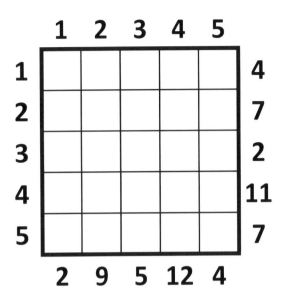

KAKURASU - 13

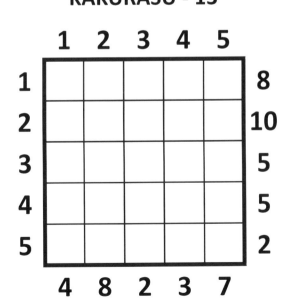

KAKURASU - 14

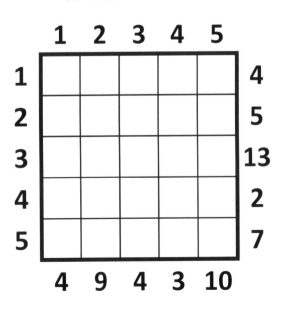

KAKURASU - 3 (Solution)

KAKURASU - 4 (Solution)

KAKURASU - 5 (Solution)

KAKURASU - 6 (Solution)

KAKURASU - 7 (Solution)

KAKURASU - 8 (Solution)

KAKURASU - 9 (Solution)

KAKURASU - 10 (Solution)

KAKURASU - 11 (Solution)

KAKURASU - 12 (Solution)

KAKURASU - 13 (Solution)

KAKURASU - 14 (Solution)

Made in the USA
Columbia, SC
17 October 2023